THE BIG PIC

PREHISTORIC WILDLIFE

GREEN ANDROID

Published by Green Android Limited,
49 Beaumont Court, Upper Clapton Road,
London, E5 8BG

Written by Lyn Coutts
Edited by Katie Wallace
Illustrated by Gilang Ayyoubi Hartanto

A CIP catalogue record for this book
Is available from the British Library

Paperback ISBN 978-1-912188-68-0

Date of Manufacture: February 2025
Manufactured by WKT Co., Ltd
Printed in China

9 8 7 6 5 4 3 2 1

Contents

Revealing Earth's prehistoric wildlife

A little more of our planet's long history is uncovered every time a fossil is unearthed, especially when that fossil comes from a prehistoric creature.

THE LAYERS OF ROCKS THAT MAKE UP EARTH'S CRUST are like the pages in a book. Every page represents a rock layer that may contain a fossil. It could be the complete skeleton of a gliding reptile that weighed 7.5 grams or the leg bone of a 73,000-kilo Titanosaur. Most discoveries are made by accident when wind, rain, ice and flowing water remove layers of sediment to expose a bone on the surface.

"I've never lost the wonder... to be the first human to find and touch an extinct creature."

Hans-Dieter Sues, palaeontologist, Smithsonian Institute, USA.

Over the last 538 million years, thousands of different kinds of animals have existed. Prehistoric wildlife includes many more creatures than just dinosaurs. There are amphibians, mammals, birds, fish, arthropods, non-dinosaur reptiles and more. You will meet some of these as you turn the pages of *Prehistoric Wildlife*. There are terrifying hunters, plant munchers, fish catchers and insect chasers. There are fangs, claws, tusks, pincers, horns, sails, wings, armour-plating, fins and flippers.

Almost all prehistoric wildlife was made extinct by catastrophes like 10-kilometre asteroids hitting Earth, volcanic eruptions, changes in climate and over-hunting by the first humans. Without the rock hammers of fossil hunters and the advanced scanners and knowledge of palaeontologists, the story of these remarkable creatures would remain unknown.

"Dinosaurs are the best way to teach kids and adults the immensity of geologic time."

Robert T. Bakker, palaeontology curator, Houston Museum of Natural Sciences, USA.

Geologic Time Scale (GTS)

The GTS is a calendar of the events in Earth's 4.54-billion-year history. Instead of days, weeks, months, the GTS has eons, eras, periods and epochs. Eons last the longest and epochs, the shortest (see page 46–47). Each panel on the chart below represents an important Earth event, like the appearance of certain life forms and their extinction. Jaekelopterus, a sea scorpion, appeared in the Devonian and Triceratops in the Cretaceous. Dinosaurs disappeared at the end of the Cretaceous and woolly mammoths in the Holocene.

Eon	Era	Period		Epoch	
Phanerozoic: Earth has abundant animal and plant life.	**Cenozoic**: new life	**Quaternary**		**Holocene**	Today
				Pleistocene	
		Neogene		**Pliocene**	
				Miocene	
		Paleogene		**Oligocene**	
				Eocene	
				Paleocene	
	Mesozoic: middle life	**Cretaceous**		~	66 million years ago
		Jurassic		~	
		Triassic		~	
	Paleozoic: old life	**Permian**		~	252 million years ago
		Carboniferous	**Pennsylvanian**	~	
			Mississippian	~	
		Devonian		~	
		Silurian		~	
		Ordovician		~	
		Cambrian		~	
Pre-Phanerozoic: during the earlier **Proterozoic**, **Archean** and **Hadean** eons, planet Earth was formed but no life existed.					538 million years ago
					4.54 billion years ago

Younger ↑ ↓ Older

~ epoch names omitted for simplicity.

Chart adapted from Jonathan R. Hendricks.

Allosaurus

Allosaurus has a well-deserved reputation as one of the fiercest Jurassic predators. From its hollow bones to its hooked claws, it was designed to hunt, catch, grip and eat meat.

LIKE ALL THE THERAPODS, Allosaurus' bones contained air sacs. These made its skeleton lighter without sacrificing strength. The air sacs increased the oxygen circulating in their blood which, in turn, gave them agility and endurance. Standing 3 metres tall and 8 to 12 metres in length, Allosaurus weighed about 2,000 kilos. It could run at speeds of 30 to 50 kph. Because of the shape of its skull, its field of vision was just 20 degrees. By comparison, the human field of vision is 210 degrees.

Allosaurus' Jurassic climate was warm and its habitat was semi-arid river floodplains with forests of tree ferns, conifers and ginkgos.

Hollow, holey skull

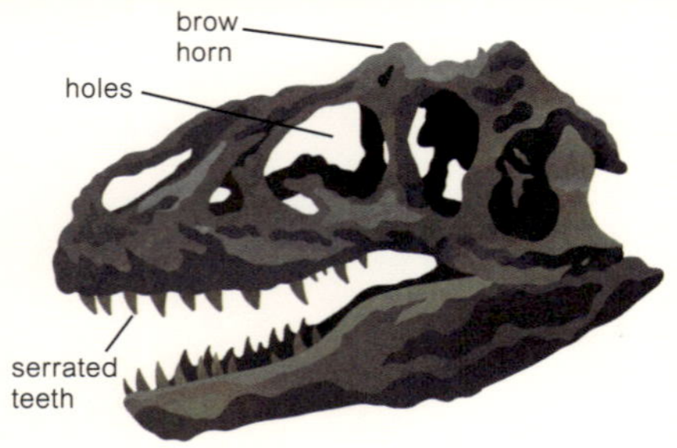

Allosaurus' skull was hollow and peppered with holes. It was 76 centimetres in length. Above each eye was a brow horn. In its jaws, 70 to 80 7.5-centimetre-long saw-like teeth curved backwards to prevent prey escaping their tenacious grip.

Size comparison

This dinosaur may have chased down its prey on strong legs or ambushed it. Once close enough, Allosaurus would grab its victim in its strong arms and skewer it with the three hooked claws at the end of each arm. Its double-hinged jaw would open very wide. Then, 70 saw-like serrated teeth would tear into the flesh. The prey would often bleed to death. Allosaurus had no cheeks so it couldn't chew. It would simply bite and swallow. Teeth were often dislodged when eating or fighting, but new teeth would replace those lost.

Each month, an Allosaurus ate its body weight in food. It may have hunted in packs to bring down larger armoured dinosaurs like Stegosaurus or injured Diplodocus. But one-on-one, Allosaurus sought out deer- and cow-sized prey like Dryosaurus, Camptosaurus and more. This therapod was opportunistic and would scavenge on carrion.

Allosaurus was formidable, but not invulnerable. Fossils show that Allosaurus incurred many injuries. There are injuries that show some prey fought back and won. One fossil clearly shows a wound caused by the tail spikes of a Stegosaurus.

Allosaurus fragilis is one of three validated Allosaurus species. The first fossil was discovered in 1877. Since then, another 60 individual specimens have been unearthed from the sedimentary rocks of Jurassic rivers, floodplains, swamps and lakes of western North America.

Plesiosaurus

This marine reptile has a snake-like neck, paddles, like the flippers of a sea lion and a turtle's broad, flat tail. This apex predator could remain underwater for an hour before surfacing to breathe air.

PLESIOSAURUS MEASURED 2.8 TO 3.5 METRES. Its neck was almost twice the length of its broad flat body and tail. Its two pairs of paddles evolved from the limbs of its land-based reptilian ancestors. It is thought the front paddles provided thrust when swimming and those at the rear steered. Plesiosaurus' small head was narrow, and the 45 to 50 long teeth in its jaws were needle-sharp. Its strong jaws had enough bite force to crack the shells of giant cephalopods such as ammonites.

This strong swimmer lived in shallow waters and may have grazed along the seabed for belemnites (soft-bodied, squid-like animals), and ammonites, clams and snails. But to catch fish, it would swim into a school of fish, swinging its head side to side on its long neck to scoop prey into its open U-shaped mouth. Plesiosaurus may have ambushed a school of fish by approaching from behind and below, much like today's great white sharks.

The first Plesiosaur fossil was found on England's Jurassic south coast in 1821. Since then, over 900 have been uncovered. Originally, it was thought all Plesiosaurs were marine reptiles, but more recent fossils have been found in what would have been freshwater during the Jurassic period. One fossil was even found in what is now the Sahara Desert. This means its diet could also have included frogs, crocodiles and turtles. In 2010, a female Plesiosaur fossil carrying an unborn offspring was found. Until then, it was thought this reptile laid eggs.

Plesiosaurus were around for about 149 million years until they were wiped out in a mass extinction event. But during their time on Earth, they evolved. Scientists have found huge differences between the skeletons of late Triassic and late Cretaceous fossils.

Plesiosaur paddles

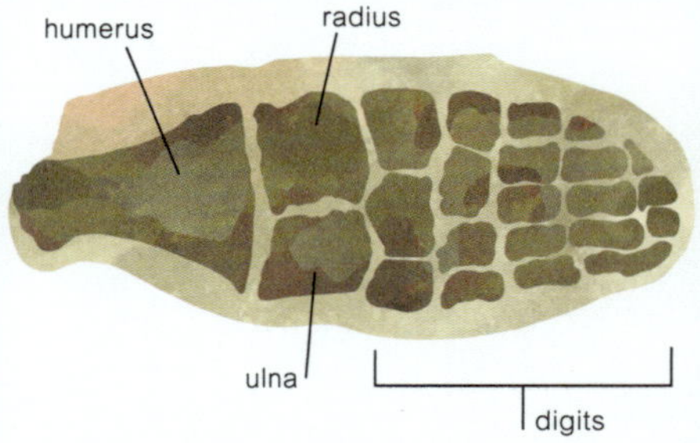

Plesiosaur paddles contain six wrist bones and five digits. The paddles could measure 35 to 75 centimetres in length. The front paddles were often larger than those at the rear. Scientists believe that the Plesiosaur's swimming motion was most like that of a sea turtle.

Size comparison

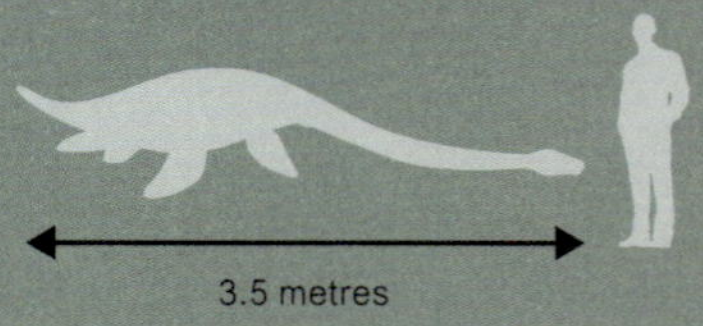

The first complete Plesiosaurus fossil was found by palaeontologist Mary Anning in 1823.

Plesiosaurus spent its entire life in water. The shallow tropical waters of the Jurassic period provided a bountiful larder for marine reptiles. There were oysters, horseshoe crabs, lobsters, fish, large snails, squid and sea urchins. Plesiosaurus ate soft- and hard-shelled prey.

Ichthyosaurus

Air-breathing primitive fish moved onto land 390 million years ago. Around 250 million years later, some of these part-fish, part-reptile creatures returned to the water. These are the Ichthyosaurs' ancestors.

THE MOST FAMOUS OF THE ICHTHYOSAURS are the seven species of Ichthyosaurus. These "fish-lizards" measured 1.8 to 3.3 metres and weighed around 100 kilos. Their torpedo-shaped body, long pointed snout, dorsal fin, paired paddles and large tail fin guaranteed speedy swimming. This globally-distributed fish inhabited shallow and deep waters. Though dolphin-like in appearance, Ichthyosaurus with their vertical tail fin have more in common with sharks and porpoises.

Air-breathing and viviparous Ichthyosaurs were tetrapods, meaning four footed. Their four paddles were modified limbs from their ancestors.

Ichthyosaurus were pursuit hunters, chasing down their prey. They located small fish, squid, shellfish, octopus, cuttlefish, ammonites, and on rare occasions birds and turtles, using smell and acute eyesight. This reptile had well developed ear bones, so may have been able to hear their prey, which would be snatched in long jaws and securely gripped by up to 200 serrated teeth.

The paired fins were used for steering. The propulsion came from the sideways movement of the tail fin. There is no doubt that Ichthyosaurus were fast, but they could not always evade the fatal bite of larger and better adapted Plesiosaurs and Pliosaurs.

In 1814, Mary Anning unearthed the first complete Ichthyosaur fossil from the limestone and shale cliffs at Lyme Regis on England's Jurassic coast. It was so complete, there were fish bones and scales from its diet inside its rib cage. Mary was only 12 when she revealed the outline of the 5.2-metre "monster". Anning was honoured 168 years after her death by having a fossil named for her: *Ichthyosaurus anningae*. All Ichthyosaurs became extinct in the mid-Cretaceous period, when climatic changes decreased their sources of food.

Largest-ever Ichthyosaur

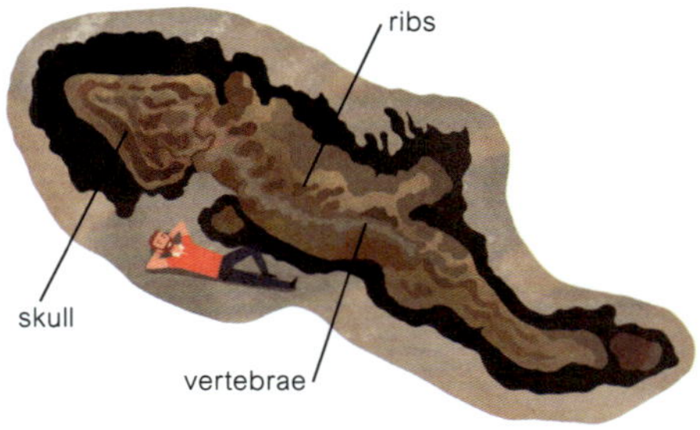

Ichthyosaurus may have measured only a few metres, but some of its relatives could grow to 25 metres. In 2021, fossil hunter Joe Davis discovered Britain's largest Ichthyosaur fossil in a drained lagoon. It was over 10 metres long and had lain undisturbed for 180 million years.

Size comparison

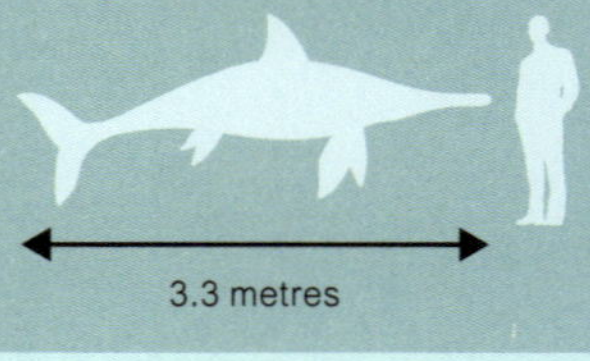

Ichthyosaurus communis lived in shallow tropical seas (in what is now Europe) during the Mesozoic era. It was built for fast, long-distance swimming. Research now suggests that some Ichthyosaurs could lighten or darken their skin colour like some modern lizards.

Triceratops

Triceratops was a tank of a beast with a large distinctive frill, long horns and huge skull. But it was not a ferocious predator of the Late Cretaceous period, just a plant-munching herbivore.

OVER 2,000 TRICERATOPS FOSSILS HAVE BEEN FOUND, so much is known about the "three-horned face" dinosaur. For a start, Triceratops lived on an island continent called Laramidia. This area is now western North America running from Alaska to Mexico. Over the last 150 years, this vast region has given up the fossils of thousands of dinosaurs. Triceratops shared this forested region with Tyrannosaurs, Dromaeosaurids, Pachycephalosaurs and other horned dinosaurs (Ceratopsians).

The sheer size of a Triceratops must have made their fossils easy to spot. It was 8 to 9 metres long, stood 2.3 metres high and weighed 6,000 to 10,000 kilos. The skull was about one-third of its total length. That means the skull measured 2 metres or more from beak to neck! If the skull alone was not big enough, add in a metre-wide bony frill and three horns – the two over the eyes could measure a metre each.

Despite its bulk, Triceratops could run at a speed of 32 kph. But speed is not important when your food can't move, and you choose to eat fibrous plants that no other dinosaur will touch. Triceratops' parrot-like beak clipped the plant; its teeth shredded and ground it ready for digestion. There was a lot of wear-and-tear on the teeth, which is why it had jaws full of teeth ready to replace any lost ones. With no competition for food and few predators (fatal battles between Triceratops and Tyrannosaurs are unproven), it is no surprise that Triceratops outnumbered other dinosaurs five to one.

The frill with is small spikes is believed to be important for courtship and dominance. The frill balloons as the animal matures, and the prescence of keratin in the frill would have made it colourful.

Fragile and rare

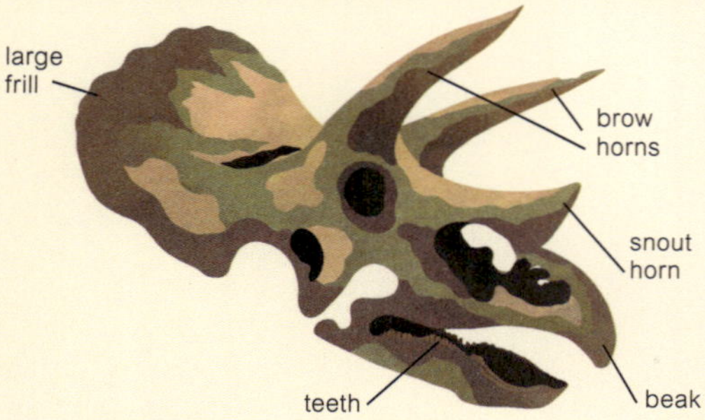

This intact skull was discovered in 1908 in Montana, USA. It was two metres long and weighed 400 kilos. Complete Triceratops skull fossils are rare. Because they are hollow, skulls are more easily crushed during fossilisation than other bones like vertebrae, femurs and ribs.

Size comparison

Jack Horner, American palaeontologist described Triceratops as being very common. They were the cows of the Cretaceous period.

There are two Triceratops species: *T. horridus* and *T. prorsus*. They grazed on low-growing vegetation like palms, cycads, gingkoes and ferns, but could easily knock over taller plants. Triceratops' footprint measured a metre across. Its horns and frill were always on display.

Velociraptor

This dinosaur earned star status in the "Jurassic Park" films. The Velociraptor seen on the big screen was 200 centimetres tall. But, the real raptor was a less-terrifying 50 centimetres.

THOUGH ONLY THE SIZE OF A TURKEY and weighing around 17 kilos, Velociraptor was a highly efficient hunter. Its main prey were small reptiles, mammals, insects and amphibians. It could run at 40 kph in short bursts on a pair of long, muscular legs. Its long tail helped to steer. Velociraptor located prey by sight, smell and sound. While this dinosaur's wing-like arms were too short for flight, they were strong enough to restrain a small mammal.

Lethal claw

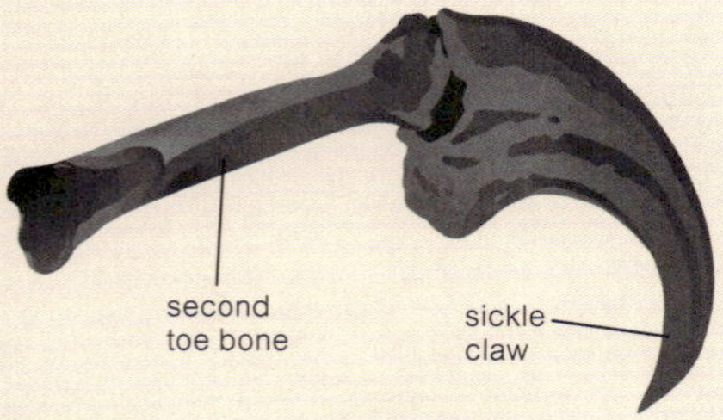

Velociraptor had four claws on each foot, and the most lethal of all measured 6.5 centimetres. This curved claw was raised off the ground so that it remained sharp. The dinosaur used this claw to grab prey and to puncture veins or vital organs in the prey's body.

Size comparison

Once near its victim, it would tackle the prey, bringing into play the sharp claws on its hands and the sharper ones on its feet. It is also likely that Velociraptor pounced onto its victim in the same way as birds of prey do. Using its weight, it would pin its catch to the ground, the lethal sickle claws impaling its prey as 60 teeth in its strong jaws ripped into the still-living flesh.

Velociraptor's brain was large for its size, but palaeontologists believe it had the intelligence of a hawk rather than a parrot, so it's unlikely that it was smart enough to be able to hunt as part of a pack.

So far over 12 Velociraptor fossils have been discovered. The first was found in 1923. One fossil shows that Velociraptor had feathers. They were not flight feathers, but could have been used to attract a mate, provide warmth or incubate eggs. The most exciting fossil captures a moment 80 million years ago when a Protoceratops and a Velociraptor were locked in combat. The Velociraptor's sickle claw is lodged in the Protoceratop's throat; its arm jammed in Protoceratops jaws. It is thought the pair died suddenly when they were engulfed by a sandstorm or in a sand dune collapse.

The Velociraptors in "Jurassic Park" were modelled on fossils of a larger but equally aggressive raptor relative, Deinonychus.

Velociraptor means "swift plunderer". This dinosaur roamed the Late Cretaceous scrublands and deserts of the Gobi Desert that covers parts of modern-day Mongolia and China. This cold desert has barely changed since the time of dinosaurs 100 to 66 million years ago.

Tyrannosaurus

The "king of the tyrant lizards" was among the largest carnivores in its Late Cretaceous kingdom. This is one prehistoric reptile that definitely deserves its reputation as a ferocious apex predator.

MEASURING 12 METRES FROM TIP TO TAIL and standing 4 metres at the hip, it weighed in at 5,000 to 7,000 kilos. Its massive head was 1.5 metres long and supported on a short but flexible neck. Though its two-clawed arms were short – so short they couldn't reach the dinosaur's mouth – they were very strong. Its muscular hindlegs were the longest in relation to body size of any theropod. The tail was long and acted as counter balance to its substantial head and neck.

Everything about *Tyrannosaurus rex* was big. One tooth and root fossil measured 30.5 centimetres, though the average tooth size was 20 centimetres. *T. rex's* jaws were equipped with 60 razor-sharp teeth. They tore off great chunks of flesh that were swallowed whole. The bite force of its jaws – three times stronger than a lion's – was enough to crush bones. This is evidenced by bone fragments in its dung.

With its keen sense of sight, hearing and smell, it could detect prey or carrion from a distance. It is believed that to keep such a huge body fed, *T. rex* couldn't be picky. It would eat live prey, scavenge on dead animals and cannibalise Tyrannosaurs it had fought and defeated. It would stalk then chase down duck-billed Hadrosaurs and juvenile armoured herbivores like Ceratopsians, Sauropods and Ankylosaurs. *T. rex's* brain was twice the size of other dinosaurs, so these dinosaurs could have had the intelligence to hunt in packs.

It is uncertain how fast *T. rex* may have been, but it was certainly not the fastest dinosaur. Some estimates are as low as 16 kph; others as high as 32 kph. For its size, Tyrannosaurus was agile and could turn and pirouette very quickly.

***T. rex*, like modern alligators, had two blood-filled vents in its skull that helped keep the reptile cool.**

Size comparison

A dinosaur named SUE

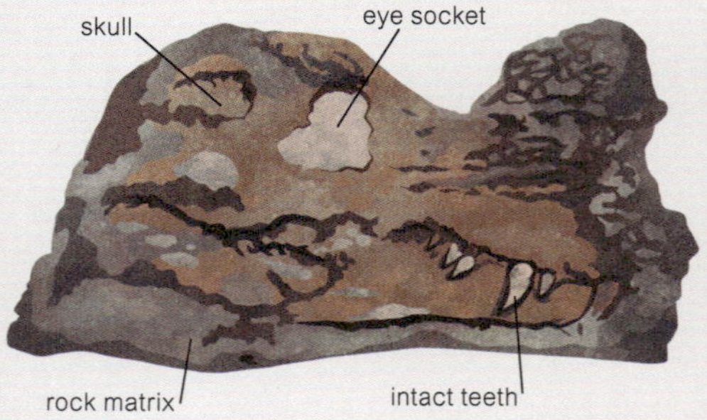

In 1990, Sue Hendrickson discovered the most complete Tyrannosaurus skeleton ever found. Of the 360 known bones in a *T. rex*, 250 bones plus the teeth were recovered. It took 25,000 hours to remove the rock that encased SUE, the *T. rex* fossil.

Tyrannosaurus lived in sub-tropical forests with high humidity. It never roamed far from the rivers and swamps that would have attracted a wide range of prey. Over 80 Tyrannosaurus fossils have been discovered, and most have been found in western North America.

Argentinosaurus

The world knows of this Titanosaur through only 13 fossilised bones. Among them is a fibula 2 metres long and vertebra that is an astounding 1.5 metres tall. Without doubt, Argentinosaurus was big!

FROM THESE MEAGRE DISCOVERIES, palaeontologists have been able to estimate that the sole species of Argentinosaurus was 30 to 35 metres in length. It stood 7 metres at the shoulder. Its mass of around 73,000 kilos was carried on four thick column-like legs. It had a very long neck and tail. The blue whale, by comparison, measures around 30 metres but weighs in at 200,000 kilos. Argentinosaurus is a Titanosaur. These long-necked sauropods included the largest land animals ever known.

Imagine the noise and vibration caused by these giants when a herd of 20 thumped across the plains!

A great discovery

In 2014 in Patagonia, in southern South America, a huge fossilised femur was discovered. From the size of the femur, this Titanosaur was 40 metres long and 20 metres tall. This animal was a sister species to Argentinosaurus.

Argentinosaurus used its peg-like teeth to strip the leaves off branches. It didn't chew the leaves – it simply swallowed them. Its long neck meant it could feed off the tallest trees, eating the leaves, seeds and fruit of the conifers it preferred. This huge eating machine ate vast quantities of plant material quickly to fuel its massive body.

Argentinosaurus was preyed on by carnivorous dinosaurs like Mapusaurus and Giganotosaurus. These two smaller predators may have hunted in packs. Unlike many dinosaurs that were solitary, scientists propose that Argentinosaurus formed herds of 20 individuals.

The young of Argentinosaurus hatched out of eggs about 30 centimetres in diameter. A clutch could have contained 10 to 15 eggs. This guaranteed that at least a few from each clutch would survive when the nests were raided by other dinosaurs. On hatching, the young were about a metre tall and weighed 5 kilos. Until juvenile Argentinosaurus attained their adult size at around 15 years old, they were highly vulnerable to predators.

Argentinosaurus is one of the largest land animals found, but the full story of this Late Cretaceous dinosaur titan will only be known when more complete fossils are unearthed.

Argentina in South America is the land of giant dinosaur fossils. When a farmer discovered the fossil of a fibula bone in 1987, he thought it was a petrified log. After two years of digging, palaeontologists found 12 more fossils and identified the species as Argentinosaurus.

Arctodus simus

The giant short-faced bear was the largest and most powerful carnivorous land mammal in its North American range during the Pleistocene epoch. Its only living relative is the spectacled bear.

ARCTODUS SIMUS, LIKE ALL BEARS, was an omnivore. It consumed meat and vegetation. This bear possessed a well-developed sense of smell to detect prey from some distance. It had the speed (up to 40 kph), strength and size (on all fours was 1.5 metres at the shoulder) to chase and restrain bison, musk oxen, deer, reindeer, horses, ground sloths and tapirs. The plant part of its diet included berries, seed cones, tree bark, cactus fruit, palm hearts and barley.

Massive skull

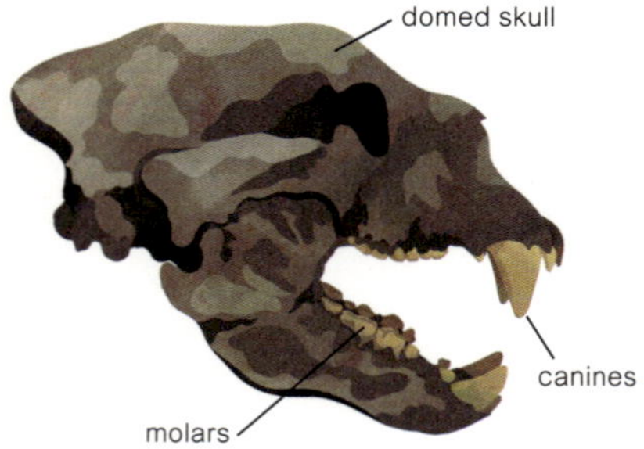

Even though called short-faced due its proportionately shorter snout, this bear's skull was up to 49 centimetres long. Its jaws had enormous bite force. It could crack the bones of hunted prey to eat the nutrition-rich marrow inside.

Size comparison

This huge bear's jaws could crush bones and its canines tear flesh. The molars chewed the flesh and ground down plants for digestion. It is believed that the short-faced bear was opportunistic and would scavenge carcasses, including mammoths. A bear that stands 2.4 to 3.4 metres on its hind legs and weighs up to 900 kilos could easily steal another predator's kill. Arctodus had long, strong fore limbs that could hold prey and reach into trees. Each paw ended with 7.5-centimetre-long claws for gripping a thrashing animal trying to escape or digging up roots from frozen soil.

There have been over 100 *Arctodus simus* finds in the USA, Canada and Mexico. Some fossils have been found in caves. These fossils could be those of hibernating bears, or of pregnant or nursing female bears denning.

The giant short-faced bear lived alongside mammoths, mastodons, bisons, camels, horses and humans. The Clovis hunted megafauna (large animals over 40 kilos), including Arctodus, with sharp flint-topped spears. It is thought that hunting by the Clovis, an ecological collapse and climate change at the end of the Pleistocene epoch caused the demise of all megafauna including the giant short-faced bear.

The false thumb on each forepaw allowed Arctodus to manipulate its food and to collect wild nuts from the forest floor.

The giant short-faced bear on its hind legs was a fearsome sight. It had few predators, a wide range of food sources and could adapt to various habitats. Fossils have been found in woodlands, subtropical forests, open plains, steppe tundra and grasslands.

Smilodon

There was nothing "smiley" about these fierce apex predators. Smilodon were precision ambush killers that prowled the planet for 2.5 million years during the Pleistocene period.

THERE ARE THREE SPECIES OF SMILODON, with *Smilodon populator* being the largest. From snout to bobbed tail it was 3 metres long, and 1.25 metres at the shoulder. Weighing between 200 and 400 kilos, Smilodon was heavier and more robustly built than a modern big cat like the African lion. Its limbs were short and muscular, and ended with retractable claws. It could leap, climb trees and dig up the burrows of small prey. Until a frozen fossil is found, scientists cannot determine Smilodon's coat colour.

Rapid canine growth

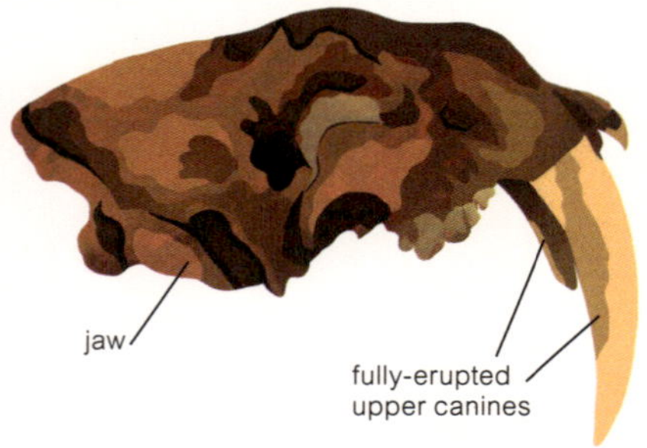

Juvenile Smilodon's milk teeth were replaced by adult teeth at 22 months old. Even though the upper canines grew at a rapid six millimetres a month, they were not fully developed until the 36th month. A parent cared for a juvenile until it had its canines.

Size comparison

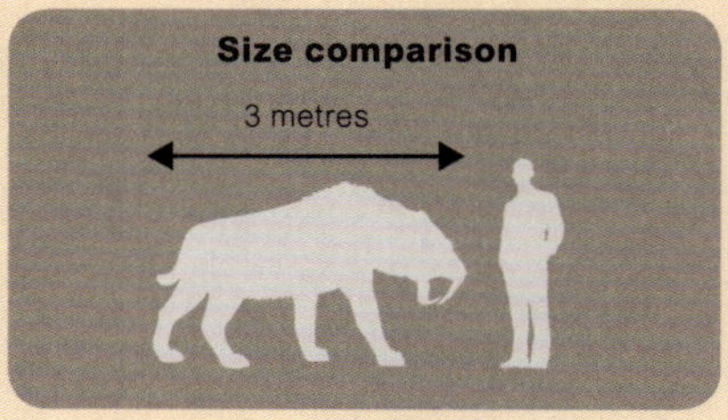

Smilodon is not closely related to any living big cats. It diverged from its ancestors 20 million years ago.

Smilodon's upper canines were essentially double-edged knife blades measuring up to 28 centimetres each. Researchers think that Smilodon stalked and ambushed its prey. It would leap on it and grip it with its forelimbs. The jaws would open to 130 degrees (a modern cat's jaws open to 65 degrees), allowing the canines to stab a vital vein or organ in the throat or stomach.

Herbivores such as horses, bison, mastodons, camels, giant ground sloths, tapirs, deer and armadillo-like animals were Smilodon's main prey. Smilodon could have been social animals. Scientists cannot confirm that they formed prides like lions, but there is fossil evidence to suggest that seriously injured Smilodons were cared for and fed until they could fend for themselves.

Over 166,000 Smilodon specimens have been discovered in the La Brea Tar Pits in Los Angeles, California. Described as the "richest palaeontological site on Earth for terrestrial fossils", this group of pits was formed by pitch seeping to the surface over the last 2.5 million years. Animals would stumble into the pits and be trapped in the sticky tar. Their distress calls attracted predators that also became trapped. The tar pits have preserved millions of animals.

Smilodon lived in pine forests, scrublands and grasslands where plant-eating prey were plentiful. It needed the cover of trees and tall grasses so that it could stalk and ambush. It is not known if Smilodon dragged its kill to a den or up into a tree to devour at its leisure.

Jaekelopterus

Before dinosaurs, reptiles and mammals ruled Earth's waters, there were the Eurypterids. Some of these armoured sea scorpions grew to an astounding size, and *Jaekelopterus rhenaniae* was the biggest.

BEFORE GETTING INTO THIS ARTHROPOD'S DIMENSIONS, there are two facts to clear up about this sea scorpion. It didn't necessarily live in the sea. Fossils have been found in what were, in the Devonian period, marine, estuarine and freshwater environments. And, Jaekelopterus is thought to have had more in common with spiders than scorpions. Now, to the exciting bit: *J. rhenaniae* measured over 2.5 metres, including its long outstretched claws.

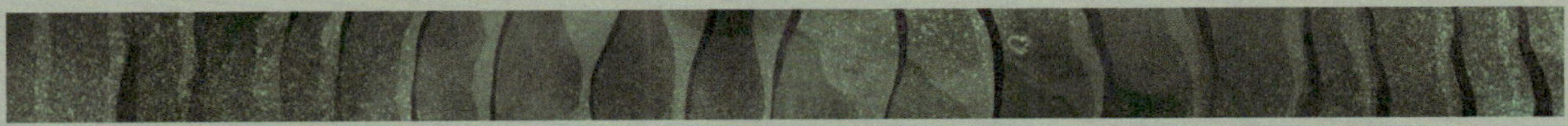

Some Eurypterids were the size of a hand. Others, bigger than an adult human. With claws at full stretch, even longer!

Evidence of the giant sea scorpion was based on a partial fossil found in a quarry in western Germany, Europe. The discovered claw was estimated to be 45.5 centimetres long, and from this scientists could work out the animal's total length. At 2.5 metres, it became the largest arthropod ever discovered. Not only were the claws large, they were equipped with well-developed teeth.

Jaekelopterus had a wide head and a body made of 12 segments. Its exoskeleton, like other arthropods, was made of strong but light chitin. The flattened tail acted as a steering rudder. The paddle-shaped pair of rear legs were used for swimming and the smaller legs for walking along the seabed. It breathed through gills and its mouth was on the underside of its head. Though not a fast swimmer, it was agile and had great vision. At the time, it was an apex predator of primitive fishes and smaller anthropods. It was not above eating its own kind.

Jaekelopterus would grab at passing prey with its long, strong and vicious pincers. It would then tear its victim into bite-sized chunks and move the pieces into its mouth. But even giants couldn't survive the Permian extinction which wiped out 81 per cent of all marine life on Earth.

Giant claw fossil

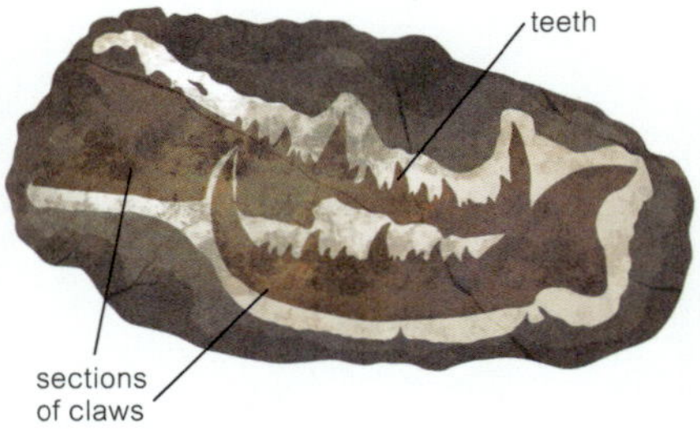

In 2007, a team from the University of Bristol, UK, were loosening pieces of siltstone in a quarry in western Germany when they spotted dark shapes. After cleaning, two sections of a large claw appeared. This fossil proved the existence of the largest known sea scorpion.

Size comparison

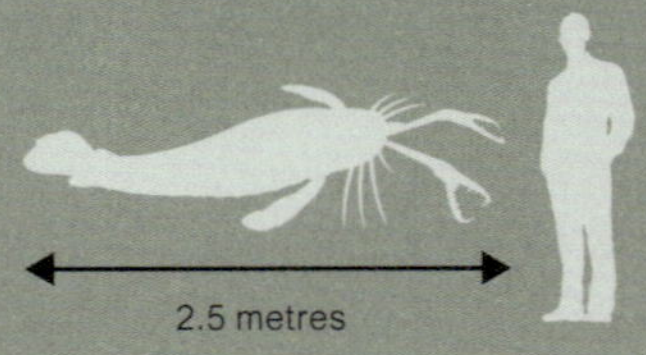

Our planet was very different in the Devonian period. There were just two landmasses in a vast ocean that covered 85 per cent of the planet. It was the Age of the Fishes. The spiky Jaekelopterus was just one of the formidable giants that flourished in the colder nutrient-rich waters.

Nemicolopterus

This robin-sized pterosaur is known from just one unique fossil. While this fossil offered another glimpse into the wildlife of the prehistoric world, it opened a can of worms for palaeontologists.

SCIENTISTS WONDER IF *NEMICOLOPTERUS CRYPTICUS* was a step in the evolution of flying reptiles like the Quetzalcoatlus or an evolutionary dead end. Until more fossils are discovered, the questions will keep coming. What palaeontologists do know is that the smallest pterosaur ever discovered had a wingspan of 25 centimetres. The skin of each wing was anchored to one long finger. There were three shorter clawed fingers on each wing. Its bird-like pointed beak was toothless.

A pterosaur laid her egg and abandoned it. The flapling hatched fully-developed, ready to fly and find food.

Unique fossil

The "hidden flying forest dweller" fossil was discovered in 2008 in northeastern China. This remarkable fossil was nearly complete, though some bones had been damaged or dislodged. It is not yet known if this fossil is a hatchling or a juvenile.

Size comparison

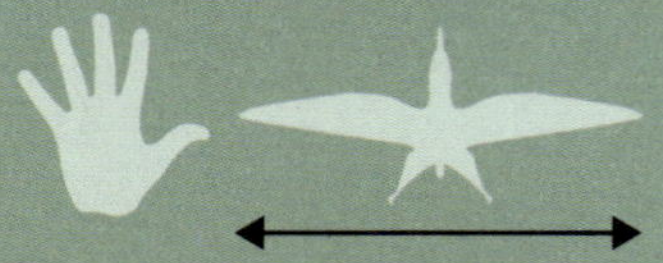

N. crypticus means "hidden flying forest dweller", and among its arboreal adaptions were curved toes and claws on its hind limbs that could grasp branches. Nemicolopterus easily moved from branch to branch, picking up insects in its beak, or could fly and catch prey on the wing. Its small size allowed it to fly easily through dense forests. Nemicolopterus might have been an omnivore, eating both insects and plants, or a pure insectivore. Its insect diet could have included beetles, flies, cockroaches, grasshoppers and dragonflies.

Sharing the forested wetlands of the Early Cretaceous period with Nemicolopterus, 145 to 100 million years ago, were predatory dinosaurs like the four-winged Microraptor and the land-based Sinotyrannus. Nemicolopterus was most likely too small and too well concealed high in the treetops to attract the attention of these hungry beasts. They needed much bigger prey.

The Pterosauria were among the earliest-known flying vertebrates, and Nemicolopterus the smallest so far discovered. Giant pterosaur "cousins" to Nemicolopterus, like Quetzalcoatlus, grew to have wingspans of 11 metres – longer than the wings on a small plane.

There is much unconfirmed about Nemicolopterus and the tiny pterosaur fossil is highly debated. Its colourings are unknown, and it may have had a crest on its head. It is certain though that it lived in dense, damp forests of ginkgo and conifers with plentiful food.

Gomphotherium

There are over 12 validated species of Gomphotherium. These beasts were a very successful early elephant that most probably gave rise to Stegodons, mammoths and modern elephants.

THE LARGEST SPECIES OF GOMPHOTHERIUM WAS 3.17 METRES TALL and weighed 6,700 kilos, making it similar in size to a modern Asian elephant. Gomphotherium had four tusks. The two on the upper jaw were longer and curved downwards. The tusks on the elongated lower jaw were sometimes shorter and curved upwards. Gomphotherium tusks were much straighter than those seen on modern elephants. The tusks, which are highly modified cutting (incisor) teeth, were round or oval in profile.

These extinct elephants had fan-shaped ears, a long trunk, thick hide and short tail. Their legs were shorter than those of modern elephants, and their molars were designed to grind tough vegetation.

It is believed Gomphotherium had few predators, but there was a lot of competition from other herbivores for roots, tree bark, leaves and branches. Their tusks could dig up roots, dislodge bark and tear down branches. The trunk would then carry the woody flora to the mouth. While the jaws moved side to side, the highly-ridged molars ground the food ready to be swallowed. Though grasses became widespread while Gomphotherium was around, this extinct mammal would have found it difficult to graze grasses with its large tusks in the way.

Gomphotherium has a fossil record of around 20 million years from the late Oligocene epoch to the early Holocene epoch. The earliest fossils were found in Africa. After an epoch of rapid evolution these mammals spread to Eurasia and North America, and finally to South America. They became extinct about 12,000 years ago. Scientists believe that Gomphotherium was not made extinct by a catastrophe, but died out because it could not adapt to a changing habitat where grasses dominated.

Florida dig site

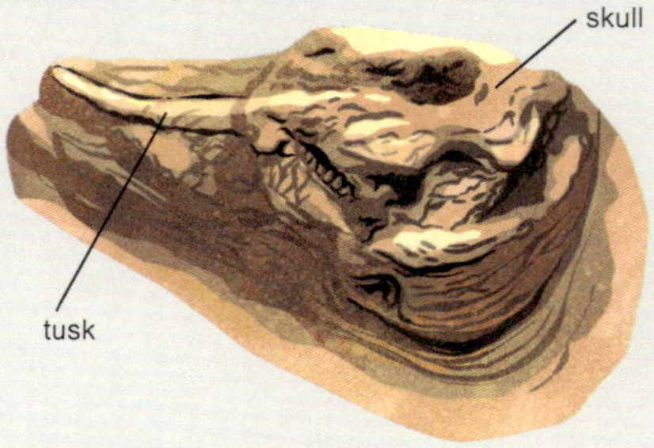

In 1915, a prehistoric graveyard was discovered at the site of an ancient river at Montbrooke, USA. Fossils of 38 individual "gomphs" and 135 other species have been discovered. It is thought animal carcasses from upstream accumulated here.

Size comparison

The upper tusks of Gomphotherium, which means "welded beast", measured around 1.5 metres.

Gomphotherium had a lifespan of 40 to 50 years. They lived mostly in forests and marshes where there was plentiful vegetation and water. It is not known if Gomphotherium were solitary, formed herds or had matriarchal-led social groups like modern elephants.

Dunkleosteus

Palaeontologists call Dunkleosteus, "Dunk". A friendly name for a fearsome fish that opened its mouth to inhale its prey, crushing it between self-sharpening plates before spitting out the bones.

DUNKLEOSTEUS WERE THE FIRST VERTEBRATE SUPER-PREDATORS. Their battering-ram-like head was armoured with five- to seven-centimetre-thick bony plates. Their large jaws could be opened rapidly. This created a suction force that pulled prey, big or small, into its gaping mouth. The jaws would snap shut with a bite force twice that of great white sharks, crushing its victim between armoured plates, sculpted into fangs and cutting edges. Its bite force is one of the highest of any animal, ever!

Much is known about the head because the thick bones formed a fossil record. There are no fossils of "Dunk's" thin armour-plated and cartilage body. Scientists estimate this predator's maximum length to be 9 metres and its top weight 3,600 kilos. Their body shape was most like that of a modern tuna or shark. They had pectoral fins.

Dunkleosteus lived in open seas around the globe. Juveniles may have stayed in shallower waters catching soft-bodied prey. When mature, they headed to deeper waters to bring the full force of their jaws down on other armoured prey, like ammonites and other placoderms. Fossils show that Dunkleosteus would even attack its own kind. It is not known if it was cannibalism or a battle over territory. One example of Dunkleosteus' regurgitated vomit contains the teeth of the larger and faster Otodus. This shows that "Dunk" was indeed an apex predator.

Pigment cells from Dunkleosteus suggest that it was camouflaged in the same way as some modern fish. The upper body was darker coloured to make it less obvious when viewed by prey or predator from above. The lower half of the body was more silvery so it would be less visible when seen from below.

Armoured and dangerous

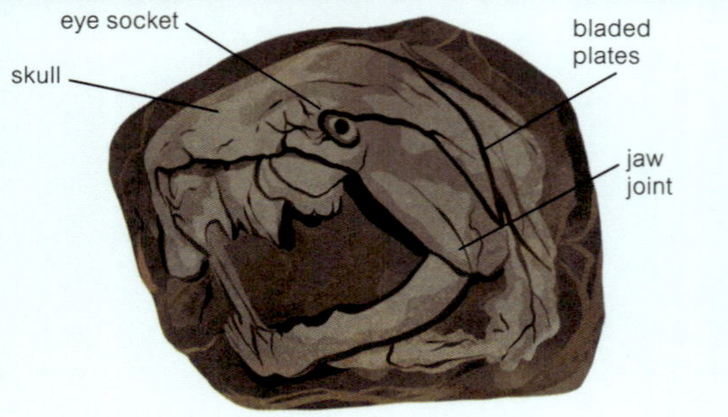

This fossil of Dunkleosteus shows the plates that made up its armoured and jointed head. If struck by this head at full force, prey would be dead or stunned. The skull of the largest fossil measured 70 centimetres. This placoderm was toothless, but those mouth plates could kill.

Size comparison

Dunkleosteus lived in the Late Devonian period until wiped out in a mass extinction event.

There are about ten species of Dunkleosteus, the largest was *D. terrelli*. Its fossilised head was discovered in 1867 in the cliffs of Lake Erie, Ohio, USA. Dunkleosteus hunted the early shark, Cladoselache. Fossils of this four-dorsal-finned shark were found near to the skull of Dunkleosteus.

Sharovipteryx

This gliding reptile is unique. Only one fossil has ever been discovered, and its wing design has never been seen on any other animal before or since. The *Sharovipteryx mirabilis* is a one-off.

MEASURING 25 CENTIMETRES FROM ITS POINTY snout to tail tip, Sharovipteryx weighed only 7.5 grams. Its narrow body was covered with lizard-like scales. The triangular-shaped gliding surface was anchored to its hind legs. This membrane of skin ran from behind its forelimbs to the tips of its wide feet. The hind legs acted like the strut on a hang-glider. Some 225 million years before the delta-winged supersonic Concorde took off, there was the tiny delta-winged *S. mirabilis*.

One of a kind

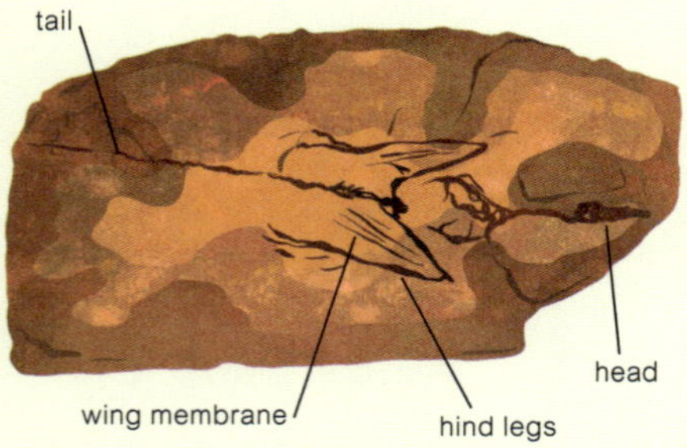

This is a cast of the unique Sharovipteryx fossil. It was largely complete and its hind limbs, delta wing, torso, head and beak are easy to see. It was discovered in 1965 in the Madygen Formation in Kyrgyzstan, which has so far produced over 20,000 insect fossils.

Size comparison

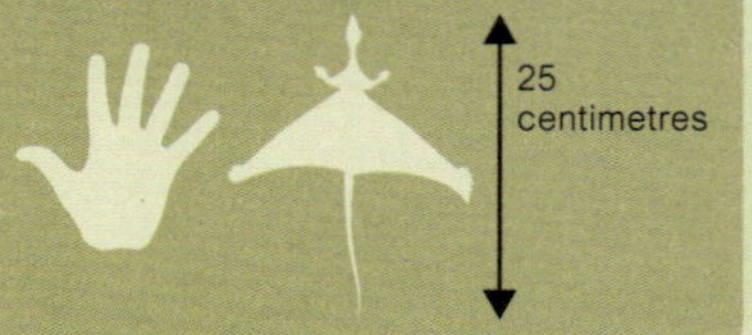

During gliding, its fore limbs stabilised flight. The tail could bend up or down to increase or decrease drag. Tension on the wing was maintained by the hind limbs. In modern gliding reptiles or mammals like Draco or a sugar glider, the gliding membrane fills the pectoral area between the forelimbs and hind legs. In Sharovipteryx, the wing surface was in the pelvic area.

Sharovipteryx' ancestors were most probably climbers not gliders. They could not walk on four limbs, but their long splayed hind limbs and five clawed toes were made for gripping and scrambling up trunks and along branches. At some point, they evolved a membrane that allowed them to glide through their densely forested habitat.

The diet of this unique species consisted of insects, and its woody, very wet and green environment was full of them. Sharovipteryx had its choice of moths, beetles, crickets, mosquitoes, flies and more. Some Triassic insects, like Gigatitans, would have provided a feast. The animals in its habitat were those suited to life in the trees. Sharovipteryx browsed for scuttling insects on branches or snatched flying ones from the air in widely-spaced, small sharp teeth.

Protorosaurs, which includes Sharovipteryx, is a genus full of evolutionary unique, oddball and bizarre Triassic reptiles.

Being able to climb and glide gave Sharovipteryx an advantage when looking for insects and evading predators. One predator could have been *Gigatitan vulgaris*, a mantis-like insect with a 40-centimetre wingspan. During courtship, this huge insect emitted flashing lights.

Josephoartigasia

The largest rodent living today is the capybara. Weighing a modest 200 kilos and just 1.34 metres in length, the capybara is dwarfed by Josephoartigasia, the biggest rodent ever found!

THERE ARE TWO SPECIES OF THIS EXTINCT RODENT, and the prize for size goes to *J. monesi*. As there is only one fossil — an almost complete skull measuring 53 centimetres — *J. monesi* is estimated to have weighed 1,000 kilos, measured 2.6 metres from nose to rump and stood 1.5 metres high. Because of its bulk, this mammal from South America has been compared to a bison. Josephoartigasia and other large rodents lived from the Early Pliocene to the Early Pleistocene epochs.

Josephoartigasia's most distinctive features were the incisors. There were two in the upper jaw and two in the lower jaw. The incisors were 25 centimetres long and incredibly strong – certainly strong enough to withstand the stress of this rodent's extraordinary bite force. The incisors could bite down with a force of 136 kilos and the molars, 424 kilos. This is similar to the bone-crunching bite of a crocodile.

The skull was reinforced to cope with the force of the jaws snapping shut to crack a nut, dig a burrow or tear roots from the ground. Josephoartigasia may have used its incisors in the same way an elephant uses its tusks.

The incisors were chisel-like and widely spaced. The teeth would grow throughout the animal's life. Alongside the incisors were molars – eight in each jaw. These smooth but slightly ridged teeth ground the plants so they could be swallowed.

While these herbivores tore, dug and munched their way through hard and soft plants, leaves, fruit, roots and aquatic vegetation, carnivores looking for lunch would have been nearby. Josephoartigasia's incisor teeth may not have been enough to scare off predators like scimitar-toothed cats, flightless terror birds and crocodiles.

Four million years ago, a giant rodent roamed Uruguay in South America. Its only living relative today is the reclusive pacarana.

Size comparison

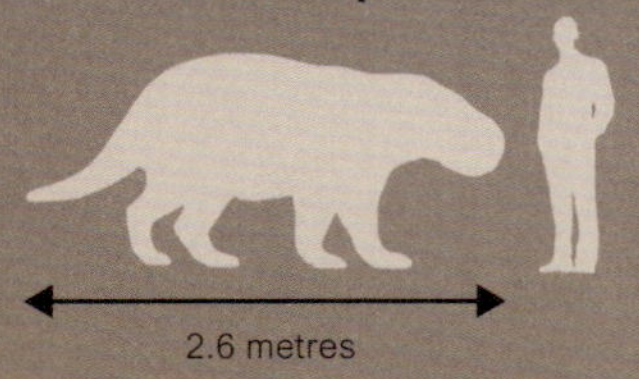

Partial skull made whole

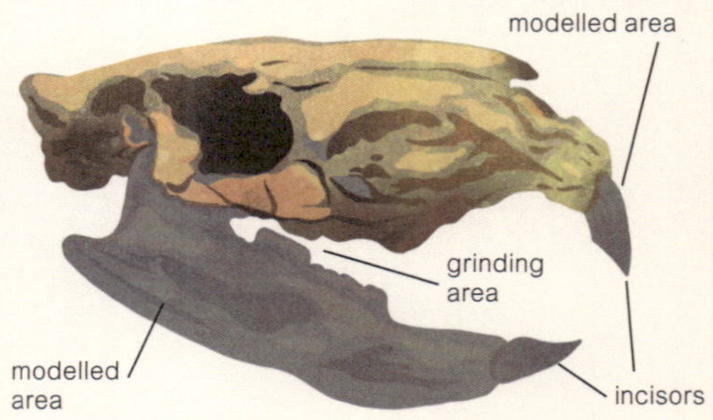

With only a partial skull of *J. monesi* to work from, palaeontologists based the modelled lower jaw on a plains viscacha, a tiny rodent. Using 3-D scanning, they got a very close approximation of the whole skull and could determine Josephoartigasia's bite force.

The handful of fossils for both *J. monesi* and *J. magna* were found in the San Jose Formation in Uruguay, South America. Palaeontologists believe that these two mammals also lived in the warm, humid forests and estuary wetlands of Argentina, Colombia and Venezuela.

Stegosaurus

What can turn a 7-metre, 5,000-kilo plant-chewing dinosaur into one of the most easily recognised of all dinosaurs? Lots of large, look-at-me plates and long lethal spikes, that's what!

ALL THREE CONFIRMED STEGOSAURUS SPECIES were heavily built with short fore limbs and long hind limbs. At the end of their short neck was a long, narrow head. The head was small in relation to the dinosaur's size, and its brain was about the size of a plum. Stegosaurus held its tail high and its head about a metre off the ground. It walked on all fours. Because its brain was small, scientists proposed that the "dummest dinosaur" had a second brain near its hips. It didn't, of course.

"Apex" is the world's most expensive fossil and the largest reconstructed Stegosaurus fossil. It sold for £34 million in 2024.

From Stegosaurus' neck to its tail were two rows of keratin-covered bony plates. The 17 to 22 plates were not attached to the skeleton, but emerged from the skin. They varied in size with the largest plates, up to 60 centimetres tall and wide, being over the back and hips.

Stegosaurus earned its name "roof lizard" because palaeontologists thought that the plates lay flat, like shingles, over the dinosaur's body. It was not until an intact fossil was discovered that they could see where the plates should be. The plates were thought to have protected Stegosaurus if attacked, but it is more likely they helped regulate body temperature or were used in courtship. On the underside of Stegosaurus' throat was a series of small paddle-shaped bones. These protected the dinosaur's jugular vein from a predator's attack.

The four dagger-sharp 60- to 90-centimetre-long spikes on the tail were purely for defence. With the tail swinging left and right, the horizontally-splayed spines would cut through the air, keeping a predator at a distance or injuring it. One Allosaurus fossil had a puncture wound that was clearly caused by a Stegosaurus tail spike.

"The Great Plate Debate"

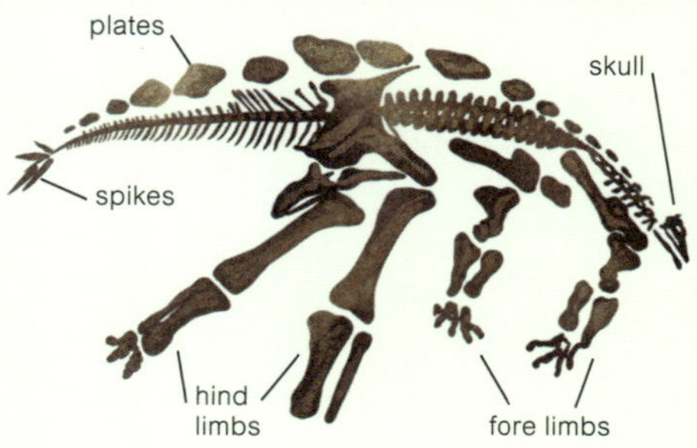

For decades, palaeontologists debated the position of Stegosaurus' plates. When a fossil proved they were upright not flat, discussion turned to one row or two, and paired or alternating. The current thinking is two rows of alternating plates.

Size comparison

In the Late Jurassic, Stegosaurus roamed floodplains browsing low-level tree ferns, fungi, mosses, conifers and horsetails. In place of front teeth, it had a horned beak that sheared leaves off branches. Plant matter was ground by small teeth at the back of the mouth.

Spinosaurus

Spinosaurus was the first dinosaur known to have swum. It is also the largest carnivorous dinosaur ever discovered. Spinosaurus was both longer and heavier than the mighty *T. rex* and Giganotosaurus.

THE FIRST SPINOSAURUS FOSSILS – teeth, lower jaw and three vertebrae with attached spines – were discovered in 1912 in Egypt, north Africa. But tragically all of the Spinosaurus fossils were destroyed in a bombing raid during World War One. It was 100 years before another Spinosaurus was found, this time in Morocco, north Africa. With limbs, pelvis, backbones, skull and 131 tail bones, palaeontologists could start to tell the story of this remarkable 100- to 94-million-year-old dinosaur.

Preference for fish

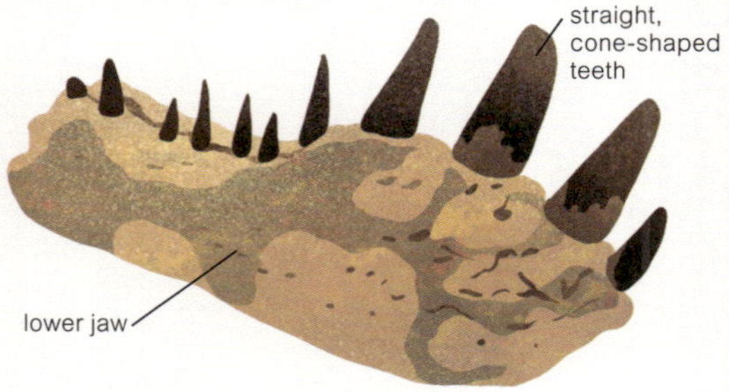

Spinosaurus' crocodile-shaped jaws were designed for catching fish. The jaws snapped shut quickly to prevent prey escaping. The front teeth were 15 centimetres long; the back 2.5 to 7 centimetres long. The teeth grasped the prey before swallowing it whole.

Spinosaurus may have hunted submerged in water, its sail corralling fish towards its fast-closing jaws or its tail lashing out to stun prey.

Spinosaurus was originally thought to be a terrestrial dinosaur that lumbered around on two short hind limbs and had a sail on its back. With more complete fossils to study, Spinosaurus turned out to be a semi-aquatic predator. It could hunt on land, and swim and hunt in water. Suddenly, the sail, flattened tail, dense and compact bones, broad flat toe bones and elongated jaw all made sense.

This semi-aquatic dinosaur was 6 metres tall, weighed 7,000 kilos and was 15 metres long. If its dimensions and large sail weren't enough to make it stand out, Spinosaurus also had a paddle-like tail. The sail was formed by neural spines that stood upright from the vertebrae. The longest spines measured 1.65 metres, and the whole sail was covered by a membrane of skin. The long tail also contained neural spines. The deep and flattened tail that could propel and steer Spinosaurus in water or could be whipped side to side to stun, injure or kill.

It is believed that Spinosaurus had few, if any, predators. Its size alone was possibly enough to deter attack, but add in the intimidating sail, gaping jaws, long claws and slashing tail, and Spinosaurus would have looked fairly unbeatable even to other similar-sized carnivores.

Spinosaurus lived on tidal flats and mangrove forests in the Late Cretaceous period. It hunted fish like coelacanths, sawfish, lungfish and sharks. In the dry season, Spinosaurus would scavenge or hunt small- to medium-sized pterosaurs and mammals.

Quetzalcoatlus

Named after the Aztec feathered serpent god, Quetzalcoatlus was the largest flying animal ever known. With an 11-metre-wingspan, it would have glided way above the heads of *T. rex* and Triceratops.

THERE ARE TWO SPECIES OF THIS PTEROSAUR: *Q. northropi* and the smaller *Q. lawsoni*. The larger species weighed 230 kilos and when standing erect was as tall as a giraffe. Its body was covered in hair-like fibres. The hind limbs and relatively small body were packed with powerful muscles. At the end of its 3-metre-long neck was a large crested skull with pointed jaws. Like modern birds, Quetzalcoatlus had hollow bones with ballon-like air sacs.

Crested skull

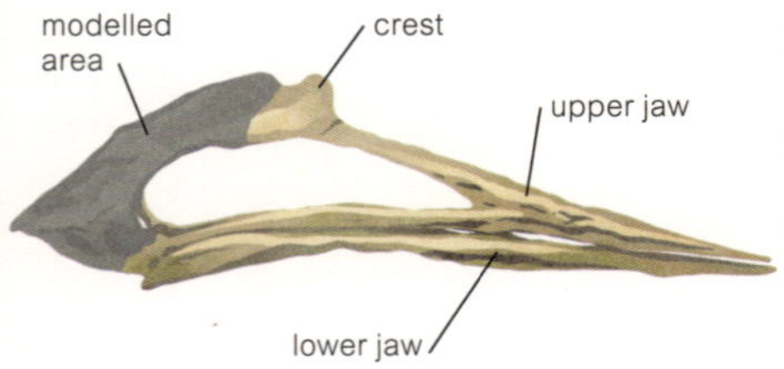

Quetzalcoatlus' skull was 3 metres long, including the 1.8-metre jaws that formed the beak. The white sections of the skull are the original fossil discovered in Texas, USA in the 1970s. The dark area is a reconstruction based on another species of pterosaur.

Quetzalcoatlus' fore limbs were elongated to create a pair of wings. Along each leading edge were three clawed digits. The fourth digit had become a giant wing finger. The wing surface was a membrane of skin. The long wingspan made Quetzalcoatlus a great glider. It is thought it could fly extremely long distances with only the occasional flap of its wings. Take-off required the animal to jump, using its powerful legs. Once 2.5-metres off the ground, the wings had sufficient clearance to flap. Landing was simply a matter of slowing its descent and planting its hind feet on terra firma.

Even with the wings folded, they touched the ground. To walk, Quetzalcoatlus would lift a wing before taking a step forward on a hind foot. Walking was important to this flying reptile. It stalked prey on land and in shallow wetlands. It would sift mud with its beak, plucking out crabs, worms, clams and fish. Its diet also included small dinosaurs, insects, snakes and lizards. It swallowed its food whole. Lack of teeth and a delicate jaw made it unlikely that Quetzalcoatlus scavenged carrion. Females made their nests in wetlands, but it is thought the eggs – perhaps as many as 12 – were buried. The female would guard the eggs for weeks.

Quetzalcoatlus glided like a modern-day condor, walked like a bat and hunted like an egret or heron.

Pterosaurs were the first animals after insects to evolve powered flight, and during the Late Cretaceous Quetzalcoatlus ruled the skies. On land, this solitary creature with an awkward walk preferred open landscapes with wetland and marshy habitats.

Woolly mammoth

Woolly mammoths disappeared only 4,000 years ago. They were still roaming the icy steppes after the pyramids at Giza were finished, and humans had invented writing and the potter's wheel.

OUR BRONZE AGE ANCESTORS WOULD have seen family groups, or even herds, of woolly mammoths foraging for grasses and sedges with their tusks and trunks. The same ancestors hunted these animals and stripped their carcasses clean. A flint arrowhead was found lodged in a woolly mammoth's rib. Other fossils show the cut marks of stone tools. Woolly mammoths were important to prehistoric people. They depicted them in cave paintings.

Adult woolly mammoths could defend themselves, but juveniles could be picked off by a pack of wolves or large felines.

Size comparison

39,000-year-old Yuka

Yuka is the mummified carcass of a young woolly mammoth. Because it was stored for so long in permafrost, the carcass is well preserved. Fur is evident on the lower limbs, the brain was almost intact and researchers could extract flowing blood.

Because of a wealth of fossils, including skin, stomach contents and more, a lot is known about woolly mammoths. The very largest males (females were smaller) would have weighed 8,200 kilos and measured 3.5 metres at the shoulder. They had highly domed heads and long trunks. Their curved tusks could be 3 metres long, and the four 24-centimetre-long ridged grinding molars could weigh 1.8 kilos each.

These animals were well adapted for their glacial environment. They could withstand temperatures as low as -45 degrees Celsius. Over a layer of fat beneath the skin were two layers of fur: 30- to 90-centimetre-long guards hairs and a shorter undercoat. Ears and tails were highly reduced in size to avoid heat loss and minimise frostbite. Fat stores in the neck and between the shoulders would have given woolly mammoths a reserve of food for lean winter months.

In 2024, researchers reconstructed the DNA from a 52,000-year-old woolly mammoth. This scientific advance reopens the debate on the possibility of recreating a woolly mammoth in the 21st century. Woolly mammoths appeared in the Middle Pleistocene. The last specimens died 4,000 years ago in the Holocene epoch.

While woolly mammoths died out in Eurasia and North America due to overhunting and climate changes, about 1,000 survived for another 6,000 years on Wrangel Island in the Arctic Ocean. If this population had avoided calamity, there could have been woolly mammoths today.

Archaeopteryx

Is it a bird? Is it a dinosaur? No, it is a transitional fossil. This means Archaeopteryx exhibits features common to birds and non-avian dinosaurs. Archaeopteryx is a bird-like dinosaur.

ARCHAEOPTERYX MEANS "ANCIENT WING" and it lived 150 million years ago in the Late Jurassic. It had a bird-like beak, a bird-like wishbone and bird-like assymetrical feathers. It also had avian hollow bones with air sacs. On the dinosaur side, Archaeopteryx had toothed jaws, a long bony tail, clawed fore limbs, extra ribs to aid breathing and hind limb "killing claws". Archaeopteryx is often called the "missing link" between dinosaurs and birds.

The bird-dinosaur that sparked a huge evolution controversy was no larger than a common raven. It was 50 centimetres long and weighed one kilo or a little less. The wings were broad with rounded ends. They had the structure and feather arrangement that would support flight. The three claws on the leading edge of each wing moved independently, unlike the fused claws of modern birds. Archaeopteryx' long tail had a row of broad feathers on each side. Its hindlegs were feathered and the second toes ended with a lethal claw. These extendable claws are the hallmark of raptors like the Velociraptor.

Extensive tests have been done to determine the colour of Archaeopteryx' plumage. The current results confirm that some, and perhaps all, of its feathers were black. According to fossil evidence, Archaeopteryx' head and upper neck may not have been feathered.

Archaeopteryx hunted during the day for reptiles, mammals, amphibians and insects. It tore into its prey with small, conical teeth. It would spot prey from a high branch or stalk it on the ground. Archaeopteryx only took to the air for short distances to evade predators or to glide onto unsuspecting prey.

Charles Darwin described Archaeopteryx as "the fossil Bird with the long tail and fingers on its wings."

Size comparison

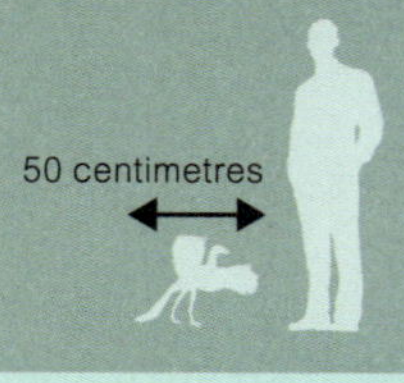

The first fossil

In 1861, the first-ever fossil of a feather was discovered in Germany. It looked like the feather of a living bird, but it was encased in 150 million-year-old limestone. It was only when five Archaeopteryx fossils were found nearby that the feather was finally identified.

Of the 14 Archaeopteryx fossils discovered, 13 were found in a quarry in Germany. Millennia ago, this quarry was a sub-tropical lagoon in a conifer forest. Archaeopteryx shared this habitat with small dinosaurs like Compsognathus, and pterosaurs, mammals and insects.

Prehistoric Wildlife word bank

ambush
To carry out a surprise attack on prey from a concealed place.

ammonite
A cephalopod with a tightly wound shell that became extinct 66 million years ago.

amphibian
A cold-blooded scaleless animal with a backbone that lives part of its life on land and in water, like frogs and axolotls.

Ankylosaurus
An extinct bulky, plant-eating dinosaur, usually with turtle-like armour, that walked on four legs.

apex predator
An animal at the top of the food chain with few or no predators.

arboreal
Everything relating to trees, especially animals that live in or rely on trees.

avian
Anything that relates to birds, and their biology and behaviour.

belemnite
An extinct squid-like cephalopod.

canine teeth
Pointed teeth that sit either side of the incisors at the front on the jaws.

cannibalise
When an animal eats the flesh of an animal of the same kind.

carnivore
An animal that feeds on the flesh of other animals.

carrion
The decaying flesh of a dead animal.

cartilage
A firm tissue in the body that connects the bones in joints and also protects the joints.

cephalopod
A marine animal with a prominent head, left to right symmetry and sets of arms or tentacles, like octopus, squid, cuttlefish and nautilus.

Ceratopsian
A plant-eating dinosaur with a parrot-like beak and bone frills, and often with horns.

Clovis people
A population of hunter gatherers that lived in the Americas 13,000 years ago in the late Holocene epoch.

coelacanth
An ancient lobe-finned fish that lives in deep water and has been around since the time of the dinosaurs. It is a living fossil.

conifer
A woody cone-bearing seed tree, like a fir, spruce and cedar.

cycad
A tree with a woody trunk topped by large, stiff evergreen leaves.

denning
When an animal, like a bear, moves to a secure and warm shelter of some kind to give birth or nurse offspring.

Draco
A genus of gliding lizards.

eon
A geological time lasting several hundred million years to two billion years.

epoch
A geological time lasting hundreds of thousands of years to tens of millions of years.

era
A geological time lasting tens to hundreds of millions of years.

evolution
The modifications and changes in the characteristics of a species over several generations.

femur
The longest bone in the body that runs between hip and knee joints.

flight feathers
The feathers that make up the wings and tail of a bird.

formation
In the study of geology, a formation is a layer of rock. In the layer, all the rock has similar characteristics.

fossil
Any preserved remains, impressions or traces of something that once lived.

fossilisation
The process whereby a fossil is preserved.

ginkgo
A seed-producing tree growing to 35 metres with fan-shaped leaves. It is a living fossil.

herbivore
An animal that eats only plants.

humerus
A long bone that runs from shoulder to elbow.

incisors
Narrow teeth at the front of the jaw used for cutting.

incubate
Keeping a clutch of eggs warm so that they hatch.

insectivore
A carnivorous animal that only eats insects.

keratin
A protein which forms tissues of the hair, nails and outer layer of skin.

mammal
An animal with a backbone that is usually covered in fur or hair. It gives birth to live young that are fed on milk produced by the mother.

mass extinction event
A widespread and fast decrease in the number and variety (diversity) of life on Earth. There have been five to twenty mass extinction events on Earth in the last 540 million years.

matriarchal
Refers to a herd or group led by a female or females.

matrix
This is the material, usually a variety of rocks, that encases a fossil.

megafauna
Any very large carnivore or herbivore.

milk teeth
The first set of teeth grown by an infant. These are shed and replaced by permanent teeth.

molar
A grinding tooth at the back of the jaws.

mummified
The natural preservation of a dead animal, including its organs and soft tissues, in an environment that is very dry or cold and lacking in air.

neural spines
Extensions from the back (spine) of an animal that forms, for example, the sail on a Spinosaurus.

Otodus
An extinct genus of mackerel sharks.

omnivore
An animal that eats meat and vegetation.

opportunistic
An animal that will consume a wide variety of prey, dead or alive.

palaeontologist
A person who studies the history and process of evolution by examining fossils.

pelvis
Bones that connect the upper body with the legs.

period
A geological time lasting tens of millions of years.

Permian-Triassic extinction
The largest mass extinction known on Earth that caused the loss of 81 per cent of marine life and 70 per cent of terrestrial life. It occurred 250 million years ago.

petrified log
When woody materials are buried in wet sediments containing minerals. The lack of oxygen slows decay.

placoderm
An extinct prehistoric group of jawed fish that were partially covered in armoured plates.

Protorosaurus
An extinct reptile from the Late Permian period.

pterosaur
An extinct group of flying reptiles.

radius
One of the two bones (the other is the ulna) in the forearm.

regurgitate
To vomit up food already swallowed.

reptile
An animal with a backbone and dry scaly skin that mostly lays soft-shelled eggs on land.

rodent
A gnawing mammal with a pair of incisor teeth in the upper and lower jaws that grow continuously throughout the animal's life.

sauropod
A group of lizard-hipped dinosaurs with a long neck and tail, small head and four pillar-like legs.

sedimentary rock
This is formed when loose sediments are deposited in lakes and oceans where they are cemented to form rocks like sandstone, limestone and shale.

sickle claw
A highly curved claw with a razor-like inner edge and sharp point.

terrestrial
Anything related to living and growing on land.

tetrapod
A four-limbed animal with a backbone.

theropod
Meaning "beast footed", this group of extinct dinosaurs have hollow bones and three claws or toes on each limb.

tibia
One of two long bones (the other is the fibula) between knee and ankle.

Titanosaur
A group of sauropod dinosaurs that includes some of the largest land animals ever known, like Patagotitan and Argentinosaurus.

ulna
See radius

validated
A fossil that has undergone rigorous study so that its classification is confirmed.

vertebra
A bone in the spine that protects the spinal cord. The spine is made up of multiple vertebra.

viviparous
An animal that gives birth to a partially- or fully-developed juvenile.

World's top fossil sites

NORTH AMERICA

Dinosaur Provincial Park, Canada
The first discovery at this site was a 70-million-year-old flesh-eating lizard. Since then, 58 dinosaur species fossils have been collected.

La Brea Tar Pits, USA
These Ice Age pits have given up sabre-toothed cats, birds, bisons, mastodons, Smilodons, *Arctodus simus* and even a female human.

Hell Creek Formation, USA
Covering 1,000 sq km in Montana, Wyoming and North and South Dakota, this Cretaceous area is king for Triceratops and *T. rex*.

Dinosaur National Monument, USA
The fossils of Stegosarus, Allosaurus and more have been found in the 800 dig sites of this Jurassic palaeontological park in Colorado and Utah.

Montbrook Fossil Dig Site, USA
Covering just 0.28 sq km, it is a Gomphotherium graveyard of the Miocene to Pliocene epochs.

Big Bend National Park, USA
The first Quetzalcoatlus fossil was found here, but the Cretaceous limestone has also preserved *T. rex*, duck-billed and horned dinosaurs, and the 24-metre-long Alamosaurus.

SOUTH AMERICA

Mene de Inciarte, Venezuela
This tar pit has produced 16,000 Pleistocene specimens from microscopic seeds to the bones of megafauna like Smilodon.

Plaza Huincul, Argentina
This small city is known for its fossils of the world's biggest dinosaurs, including Argentinosaurus, Giganotosaurus and Mapusaurus.

Talara Tar Seeps, Peru
The Pleistocene fossil record of these pits includes giant armadillos, ground sloths and jaguars, dire wolves and many species of birds.

Raigón Formation, Uruguay
This area has produced Pliocene to Middle Pleistocene fossils of Josephoartigasia, rhino-like herbivores, ground sloths and terror birds.

EUROPE

Messel Pit, Germany
This disused quarry is a World Heritage site. It contains Eocene fossils, many of which retain skin impressions, fur and feathers.

Solnhofen Limestone, Germany
The fine-grained limestone at this site preserved the fragile bones of Archaeopteryx. It has produced the fossils of over 600 Jurassic species.

Jurassic Coast, England
This World Heritage site runs for 153 kilometres. Its limestone contains Ichthyosaurs, Plesiosaurs, ammonites and more.

ASIA

Western Liaoning District, China
Known as the "Park of the Cretaceous", the first feathered dinosaur (Sinosauropteryx) and the unique Nemicolopterus were found here.

Flaming Cliffs, Mongolia
The Gobi Desert's arid conditions preserved the fossils of Protoceratops, Velociraptors and Oviraptors. Dinosaur eggs were first discovered in the cliff's Cretaceous red sandstone.

Madygen Formation, Kyrgyzstan
Best known as the most prolific Triassic insect fossil site in the world, it has also preserved fish, amphibians and reptiles like Sharovipteryx.

River Berelekh, Russia
This area has yielded 10,000 mammoth bones and 200 complete woolly mammoth fossils. This mass burial is from the Late Pleistocene.

OCEANIA

Riversleigh Fossil Site, Australia
Many of the Oligocene to Miocene fossils of birds, mammals and reptiles found here retain their 3-D shape as they were formed in soft limestone.

AFRICA

Kem Kem Fossil Beds, Morocco
The population of this area was 70 per cent predatory 101 to 94 million years ago. Predators included Spinosaurus, Plesiosaurs, armoured fish and shark-toothed lizards, Carcharodontosaurus.

Karoo Basin Supergroup, southern Africa
Covering 400,000 sq km, this is the largest fossil collecting area in the world. The sedimentary layers represent 120 million years (Permian to Jurassic) of Earth's history. It is well known for its mammal-like reptile (therapsid) fossils.

Earth's changed geography
Today's deserts could have been in prehistoric times oceans or lakes. This is why some marine and freshwater fossils are discovered in the Sahara Desert or the rugged mountains of North America.